by Dara Foster

SCHOLASTIC INC.

New York   Toronto   London   Auckland
Sydney   Mexico City   New Delhi   Hong Kong

Photo Credits

Cover: Petagraphs; author photo by Jonathan P. L. Spooner.

Interior pet photos: TM 2011 PupStyle. All Rights Reserved. All photos by Jonathan P. L. Spooner except pages 29, 31, 57, and 59.

All fashion styling and photos on pages 29, 31, 57, and 59 by Dara Foster.

Interior background photos: p. 3: © Antonina Vincent/istockphoto; p. 7: © Marjan Laznik/istockphoto; p. 11: © Jeremy Edwards/istockphoto; p. 15: © Pedro Castellano/istockphoto; p. 19: © ballonguy/iStockPhoto.com; p. 23: © Cat London/istockphoto; p. 27: © Nikita Sobolkov/istockphoto; p. 35: © James Steidl/istockphoto; p. 38: © Marinini/istockphoto; p. 39: © Marinini/istockphoto; p. 43: © Roberto A. Sanchez/istockphoto; p. 47: © Raul Taborda/istockphoto; p. 51: © Ingmar Wesemann/istockphoto; p. 55: © Redmal/istockphoto; p. 63: (starry night background) © Narvikk/istockphoto, (blanket) © Tony Campbell/Shutterstock.

Special thanks to Parrieo NY & DoggieCouture.com, WoofLink, Le Petit Puppy, and Carlene Mahanna.

ISBN 978-0-545-28500-1

12 11 10 9 8 7 6 5 4 3 2 1   11 12 13 14 15

Printed in Malaysia 106
First printing, January 2011

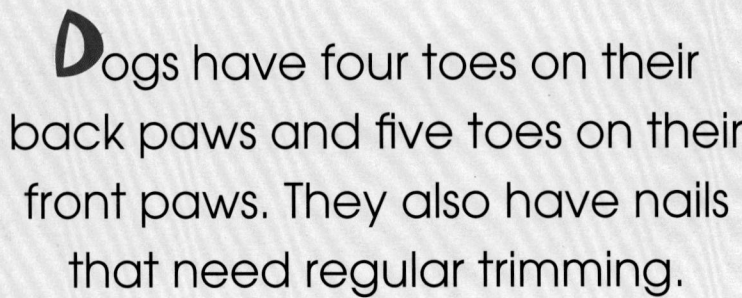

Dogs have four toes on their back paws and five toes on their front paws. They also have nails that need regular trimming.

Bulldog

This princess hopes to rule her kingdom forever. The oldest dog ever recorded lived to be over 24—that's like a 100-year-old human!

Bulldog

Even if a puppy begs for sweets, it is never a good idea to give them chocolate. When a dog deserves a snack, doggy treats are the best!

Papillon

Dogs have about 1,500 taste buds. Humans have closer to 9,000. Even though they have fewer taste buds, yummy treats still taste delicious to dogs!

Some dogs go beyond being man's best friend and perform helpful tasks. These dogs are called working dogs. Even though they're hard workers, they like to play, too.

American Pit Bull Terrier

Police dogs are a special kind of working dog. Their strong sense of smell and powerful bodies can aid police. Look out for those *paw*-cuffs!

American Pit Bull Terrier

When it comes to distance, a dog's sense of hearing is about four times better than a human's. Dogs can also hear some sounds that humans cannot.

Flat-Coated Retriever

Dogs make all sorts of noises. They bark, growl, whine, and howl. It's music to our ears, except before the sun comes up!

When it is warm outside, it is great for dogs to take walks and enjoy the fresh air. But make sure they have plenty of water!

Short-Haired Chihuahua

Some dogs can get sunburned just like humans. Dogs without fur on their bodies need to wear doggy sunscreen, or stay out of the sun completely. What dog loves the sun the most?
The Dach-*sun*!

Short-Haired Chihuahua

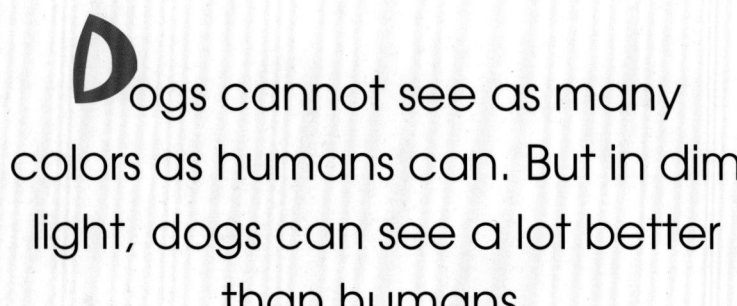

Dogs cannot see as many colors as humans can. But in dim light, dogs can see a lot better than humans.

Wheaton Scottish Terrier

Ahoy! Dogs rely on their strong sense of smell to sniff out situations. Some dogs can follow scent trails that are a few days old.

Wheaton Scottish Terrier

34

Like humans, dogs are not born with teeth. At about three weeks old, their baby teeth start to grow. It's during this time that most couches get chewed up!

Long-Haired Chihuahua

After about six months, a dog will lose its baby teeth and grow adult teeth. Most dogs have 42 adult teeth. Time for the doggy tooth fairy to pay a visit!

Long-Haired Chihuahua

Dogs need clean, fresh water every day. Water is a very important part of a doggy diet, especially on a hot day.

Pomeranian

The doggy paddle isn't just for humans. Some dogs love swimming! Other dogs have a hard time learning to swim.

Pomeranian

42

It's chow time! How much food a dog eats depends on the size of the dog. Large dogs need to eat more food than smaller dogs. Most dogs eat once or twice a day.

Dachshund

Do not pass the ketchup! Dogs may beg for food at the table, but some people food can be unhealthy for dogs. Avocados, onions, and grapes are not good for dogs. It's best to stick to doggy food!

Dachshund

Dogs have very rough pads on the bottom of their paws. When there is snow on the ground, they do not get as cold as humans in bare feet.
What dog likes winter best?
A *chilly*-dog!

Miniature Schnauzer

Some dogs have a winter coat to protect them from the cold air outside. Other dogs need to wear a jacket to keep warm. Time to hit the slopes!

Miniature Schnauzer

Dogs have many ways of communicating how they feel. When dogs are scared, they may put their tail between their legs.

Chinese Crested

When dogs are happy, they will energetically wag their tails. When dogs sense danger, they will bark. One way to keep dogs feeling groovy is by giving them lots of belly rubs!

Chinese Crested

Dogs are certainly smart pets. They can learn tricks, and sometimes even outsmart their owners!

Jack Russell Terrier

Dogs like the Jack Russell Terrier are known for their brainpower. Some dogs can even be movie stars because they can follow commands better than the rest.

Jack Russell Terrier